The Story of Diane the Turtle

A True Story

and the boy who grew up with her

Written by Jim Tonner

Illustrated by Brad Tonner

ISBN-13: 9780997412567

This book is dedicated to our Father, who took care of Diane the Turtle for many years. At bedtime, if Diane was sunning herself, he would leave her light on. In the middle of the night we would hear him walking down the hallway to Diane's room. We could hear him say "goodnight Diane" and gently turn off her light.

BRAD TONNER

The Story of Diane the Turtle

and the boy who grew up with her

Written by Jim Tonner
Illustrated by Brad Tonner

Once upon a time
and a very long time ago,
there was a little boy
named Jimmy.

The doctor told Jimmy
he had to stay in bed.

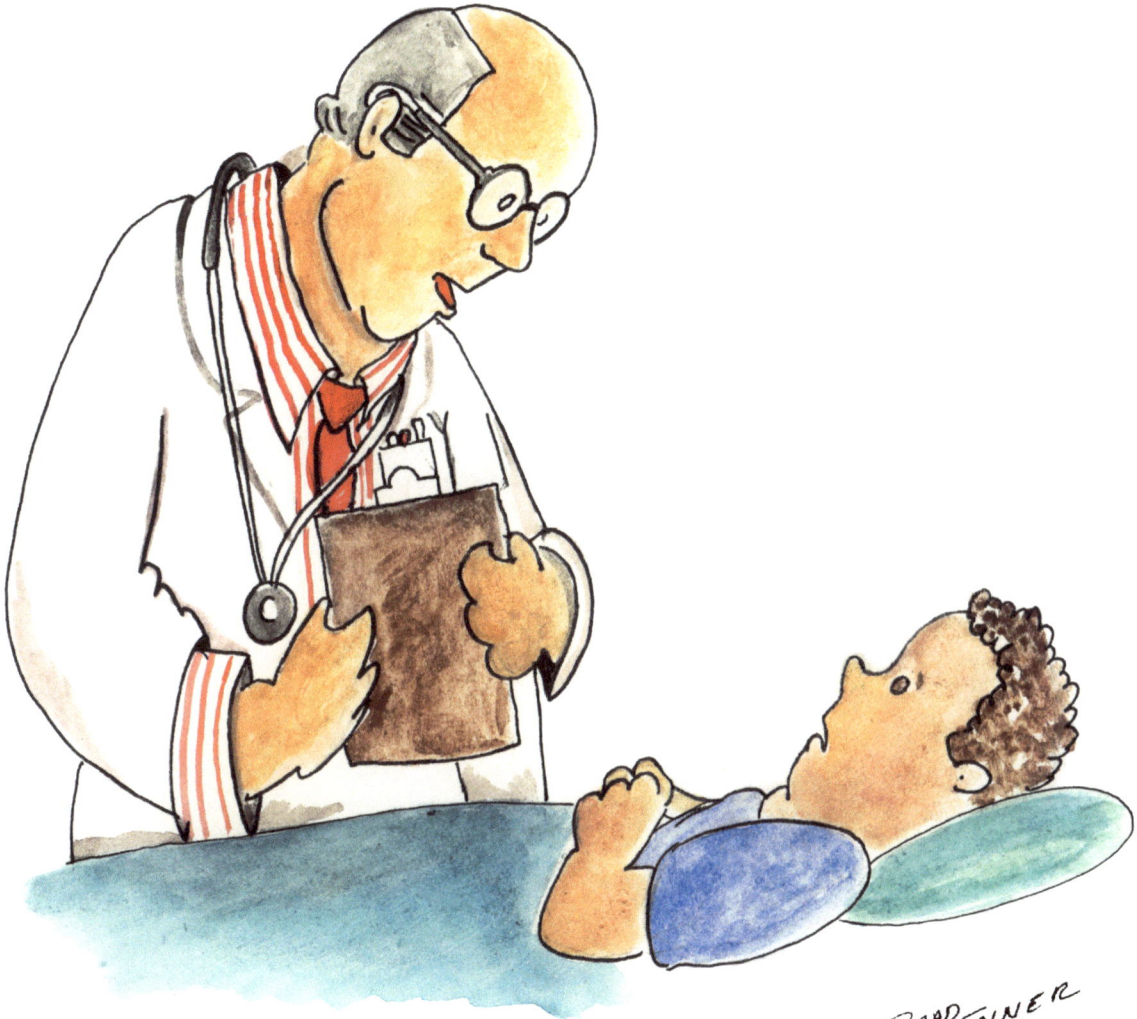

For fun, as he lay in bed,
he would drop a small basket
out his window on a string.
People would see Jimmy's basket
and put fun things inside.

One day Jimmy pulled up
the basket and you know what
he found?

A turtle!

He was so excited!
He always wanted to have a turtle for a pet.
He named her Diane after his cousin.

Diane was very small and she
lived in a plastic bowl with
a green palm tree.

One day Jimmy's dad surprised him with a much larger aquarium for Diane. Jimmy was so happy and Diane loved her new home.

Jimmy was soon all better and could once again go out and play. He would come back from his adventures and tell Diane all about them.

Diane and Jimmy
got bigger and bigger.

BRAD TONNER

And bigger!

Diane continued to grow.
She was very excited when
Jim and his twin brother Brad
got her an even bigger aquarium.

After school Jimmy would come home, clean and take care of Diane.

Diane was becoming so big that Jimmy bought her a new aquarium. It was so large that it had to be delivered by truck.

Diane's room was on the second floor.
On cleaning day Jimmy would be
up with Diane and put the hose out
the window. Brad would be down on
the lawn. Their Father would connect
the hose to the faucet. It was a lot of work
to take care of her.

But it was fun too!

Over the years Diane watched Jimmy grow up. She was very proud of him when he graduated from high school.

One day Jimmy went to Diane.
He said he would like to be called Jim
and it was time for him to go off to college.

Jim was worried about leaving Diane.
His mother and father loved Diane
and told him they would be happy
to care for her while he was away.

Jim's Mother and Father had a
wonderful time with Diane.
His mother would make
her special treats.

His father would decorate her aquarium. When she was sunning herself, he would leave her light on long into the night.

When Jim graduated from college,
Diane was there to cheer him on.

When Jim found his first job.
Diane was there to wish
him well.

Diane was included in every holiday and family gathering. Every December 15th Jim had a birthday party for Diane.

She was truly part of the family.

One day Jim brought home a friend
to meet Diane. Her name was Kelly
and it was love at first sight
for all of them.

Jim and Kelly were married on a beautiful June day. Diane was so excited about all the new adventures she would have with them.

Jim, Brad and Kelly
started a company called
TwinDesigns. Diane was there
to cheer them on.

One day they came to Diane
and told her they were opening a
store in a small New Hampshire town.
She was going to live in the store
so she could be close to them all day long.

Diane was worried about moving away from
her friends to a new place where she
didn't know anyone.

Jim and Brad decided to
celebrate Diane's 45th birthday by
having a party at their
store for her.

Some people questioned them and shook
their heads about having a birthday party
for a turtle. After 45 years together they
knew that Diane deserved a wonderful
party to celebrate.

So, that is exactly what they did!
On a December day they had a birthday party for Diane.
People came from far and wide to celebrate.
They brought balloons, cookies and there
were smiles on everyone's faces. Diane, Jim and Brad
found out that day, from old friends, new friends
and some strangers too,
that to celebrate a lifetime of love
is indeed a wonderful thing.

The best part of this story,
It is all true.

Diane the Turtle's 45th Birthday Party
TwinDesigns Gift Shop   Bristol, New Hampshire

Everyone signed her Birthday Card.

www.ingramcontent.com/pod-product-compliance
Lightning Source LLC
Chambersburg PA
CBHW042014090426
42811CB00015B/1641